BYZANTINE ART
IN ROUMANIA

Saint Athanasius' Icon.

Lavra Monastery, Mount Athos.

Copied by D. Ioldasi.

BYZANTINE ART

IN ROUMANIA

By MARCU BEZA

NEW YORK

CHARLES SCRIBNER'S SONS

LONDON & MALVERN WELLS: B. T. BATSFORD LTD.

1940

PUBLISHED SPRING
1940

MADE AND PRINTED IN GREAT BRITAIN
FOR THE PUBLISHERS, B. T. BATSFORD, LTD.,
BY WILLIAM CLOWES AND SONS, LTD., BECCLES

TO
HIS MAJESTY KING CAROL II
OF ROUMANIA

Archimandrite Kiriacos.

*Keeper of the Holy Sepulchre's Treasury, with
some of the Roumanian objects in his care.*

X

FOREWORD

BY THE ANGLICAN BISHOP IN JERUSALEM

St. George's Close,
Jerusalem.
29th January 1938.

Dear Consul-General,

On many occasions you have been enabled to interpret the mind of one people to another : to your countrymen in Roumania you have brought a fresh insight into British culture and institutions ; to your many friends in London, besides those who attended your lectures at King's College, you have thrown much light on Roumanian thought and ways ; and in one of your lectures in Jerusalem itself in the presence of an international audience you have traced the development of the Church of England.

In this your office as an interpreter of one people to another you have rightly based your work on the affinity of their religious beliefs and practices, and to this no better supplement can be given than that of this book. I know of no similar work in English. Your Roumanian edition is one of my treasured possessions, and has provided me with a knowledge of Byzantine history and art which I never possessed before, and which has largely been brought to light by your own researches.

We have both of us followed with interest the proceedings of the Conference at Bucharest in 1935, and the discussions which took place there, in the hope that

xi

ultimately full dogmatic agreement may be affirmed between the Orthodox and Anglican Communions. But the discussion of doctors and theologians of the two Churches can only attain the *rapprochement* which is our common desire if they be accompanied step by step with a mutual understanding by the laities of the two Churches of each other's art and worship and devotion.

Your beautiful volume is one of the first productions in English issued by a member of the Roumanian Church after this Agreement, and is indeed in itself a fitting commentary in art, with an introduction amplified by admirable notes of the widespread influence of the Church in Roumania and of its contribution expressed not only in goodness, but in beauty upholding the truth.

That this book should have been woven as it were on a Palestine loom of to-day from treasured patterns of several centuries is most significant, and I trust that as it goes forth from the Holy City, the birthplace of the Christian Church, it may be indeed the interpreter of various aspects of the Christian Faith, and increase the cordial relations within her fold.

It is a happy coincidence that your work *Byzantine Art in Roumania* has been largely prepared in the year of the Coronation of His Majesty King George VI, with all its religious symbolic meaning : I have every hope that members of the Anglican Communion throughout the world with minds thus inspired will be ready for this reproduction of Sacred Art and will also note with due appreciation and gratitude the gracious favour granted you in your travels and researches by His Majesty King Carol II.

> Believe me to be,
> Yours faithfully,
> George Francis,
> Anglican Bishop in Jerusalem.

The Consul-General of Roumania,
    Jerusalem.

PREFACE

THE title BYZANTINE ART IN ROUMANIA is too widely comprehensive, and I feel bound to explain that I shall treat the subject solely in the light of a number of ecclesiastical objects, hitherto unknown, which I discovered in various monasteries, libraries, and museums of the Eastern Orthodox countries, from Mount Sinai to the Highlands of Thessaly and from Alexandria through the Aegean Isles to Istambul. Both travels and researches upon such an extensive range I could not have accomplished had I not been favoured by the high support of His Majesty King Carol II of Roumania. Therefore to him, to his deep knowledge and appreciation of Roumania's past, I dedicate this book, as I did my larger Roumanian edition.

M. B.

JERUSALEM.

ACKNOWLEDGMENT

To Princess Anne-Marie Callimachi and to Mr. D. D. Dimancescu, my grateful thanks are due for their valuable help on various points of nomenclature connected with the reading of the proofs of this work.

For the photographs I am indebted to Mr. S. Schweig of the Jerusalem Museum and to Mr. Leonidas Apostolopoulos of Athens. When for one reason or another photographs could not be taken, I asked for exact copies to be made by my friend D. Ioldasi, a well-known painter in Athens.

M. B.

JERUSALEM.

CONTENTS

LIST OF PLATES

COLOUR

xvii

LIST OF PLATES

MONOCHROME

xix

INTRODUCTION

FROM the very beginning of their history, save for a brief period of no great import, the Principalities of Wallachia and Moldavia were connected with Byzantium, especially on the religious side. The metropolitans of both provinces used to be appointed by and be dependent upon the Patriarch of Constantinople. In 1373 there had been appointed to the Wallachian see a most zealous monk, called Hariton, an inmate of Mount Athos. His presence in Wallachia had helped to increase the interest that had already been taken by the Roumanian princes towards the holy Athonite establishments. Soon the Koutloumoush became almost a Roumanian monastery. A grant of money was made in 1429 by Alexander the Good to the Zographou Monastery, which another Moldavian prince, Stephen the Great, calls in a chrysobull "our monastery of Mount Athos".

After the downfall of the Byzantine Empire it was to the Roumanian rulers that passed the task of looking after the religious communities, not only of Mount Athos, but of the whole Eastern Orthodoxy. To them appealed now and again the patriarchs and the various bodies of monks in case of difficulties. Once, when the Greeks were in danger of losing the Holy Places on account of the heavy debts in which the latter were involved, the Patriarch Theofan appeared at Iassy early one morning before the Prince Basile Lupu with a piece of rope in his hand, saying : "My son, strangle me yourself, that I should not be strangled by the creditors!" The pious prince understood and gave him not only a big sum of money, but also a number of costly presents.[1] Recording the fact, Dosoftei remarks in his book *About the Patriarchs of Jerusalem* : "Since the loss of Constantinople nor king or

---

[1] The Patriarchate Codex S. Crucis in Jerusalem, No. 56, pp. 321–39.

I

prince had done such good to the Patriarchal Throne of Jerusalem."[1] Again Dosoftei wrote to the monks of Jerusalem concerning the contribution of Prince Sherban Cantacuzene for the building of the Holy Sepulchre's church : "Be glad that in such hard times alms are given to the Church of Christ."[2] I found at the library of Mar-Sabba a notice upon a book to the effect that the monastery could not open its doors but for the "insistent intervention of the Wallachian Princes". There is also in Mar-Sabba a manuscript letter of thanks addressed by the monks to the Princess Ruxanda of Moldavia for her great kindness towards that monastery. In 1570, Sultan Selim of Turkey having brought about the sale of properties of the Dokiariou Monastery in Mount Athos, it was the same Princess Ruxanda who paid for their entire redemption.[3]

These are only a few examples of the religious Roumanian generosity which reached its high-water mark in the reign of Constantine Brancovanu. He considered himself as the direct heir of the Byzantine splendour and tradition ; hence the upholder of the Christian orthodox faith throughout the Eastern world. I saw at the metropolitan residence of Aleppo the place where there stood once the printing-press presented by Prince Brancovanu and where numerous books were published for the benefit of the Christian population in Syria.

The donations in land, money, and gifts continued unceasingly through the successors of Brancovanu—the Ghicas, the Mavrocordatos, the Mavroghenis, the Sutzos, all of them God-fearing enlightened princes ; whilst the Moldo-wallachian pilgrims used to proceed along to the Holy Shrines in numerous groups, constituting more than others, as Patriarch Nectarie said, "the felicity" of the Greek monks. I often thought how overwhelmingly strong their faith must have been, in order to venture themselves towards Jerusalem in those times when the journey in itself was very wearisome and beset with unaccountable dangers. In 1844 Alexander Kinglake met such a group of pilgrims at a caravanserai in Gaza :

"Whilst I lay near the opening of my cell, looking down into the court below, there arrived from the desert a caravan—that is, a large assemblage of travellers.

[1] p. 1910.
[2] ῾Η ᾽Ιερουσαλημ καὶ τὰ Μνημεία Αὐτῆς, by Timothei Themeli, T.B., pp. 115-116, Jerusalem, 1932.
[3] Codex No. 1 of Dokiariou Monastery.

It consisted chiefly of Moldavian pilgrims, who, to make their good work even more than complete, had begun by visiting the shrine of the Virgin in Egypt, and were now going on to Jerusalem. They had been overtaken in the desert by a gale of wind, which so drove the sand, and raised up such mountains before them, that their journey had been terribly perplexed and obstructed and their provisions (including water, the most precious of all) had been exhausted long before they reached the end of their toilsome march. They were sadly wayworn. The arrival of the caravan drew many and various groups into the court. There was the Moldavian pilgrim with his sable dress, and cap of fur, and heavy masses of bushy hair . . ."[1]

Long before, a Roumanian boyar, Michael Cantacuzene, pushed his way farther down to Mount Sinai. And in memory of this devoutly desired journey he erected a monastery on the slopes of the Carpathians, where, as he says in the foundation-chrysobull, "before its building there were hermits". One of them caught once in his dream the singing of angels and amidst the divine music he saw a host of boys dressed in white with lighted candles ascending from the valley. The boyar Cantacuzene, having heard of the vision, erected on that same spot his monastery. Even this legend is but the adaptation of one amongst many that were evolved out of the leisurely uninterrupted peace of Mount Sinai.

A deep religious feeling prevalent over the Roumanian provinces urged the monks to busy themselves with manuscripts in the cloisters, and the princesses as well as the ladies of high society, to embroider sacred images for the use of Eastern churches. To the good-heartedness of the latter would come from time to time a humbly requesting message, such as the one received by Princess Smaragda Ghica from the Patriarch of Antioch, dated November 1752 :

> "The father confessor is asking Your Highness nothing else but a silver
> Gospel and a chalice of Brashov craftsmanship . . ."[2]

The valuable objects, either sent from Wallachia and Moldavia or brought directly by representatives of the monasteries, might be divided into six categories :

[1] *Eothen*, The Temple Classics Ed., pp. 173-4.
[2] *Codex Sylvestrus,* Patriarchate of Damascus.

3

I. ALTAR CROSSES AND HOLY-WATER VESSELS.

1 *Gilt bronze cross* with minute sculptured scenes of the New Testament. On its base, the emblem of Moldavia and the initials of Istrati Dabija Voevod.[1] Second half of the XVIIth century.

2 *Wooden cross,* carved in the manner of Mount Athos ; dated 1776.

3 *Another wooden cross,* richly overlaid with gold and precious stones. Sent by Costandie, Bishop of Buzau ; 1806.

4 *Large holy-water vessel* in silver, with gold applications, showing conspicuously on the front an auroch's crowned head, the emblem of Moldavia. Slavonic inscription of the donor : George Stephen Voevod, 1656.

II. LITURGICAL FANS. *Ριπίδια.*

5 *Pair of liturgical fans,* both alike, in gilt silver. On one side Christ enthroned surrounded by a Slavonic prayer ; on the other, the Holy Trinity with an inscription again in circle, which says that the fan was given by Peter Voevod and his son Radul Voevod· On the lower part are seen the portraits of the donors.

6 *Liturgical fan* in gold filigree, ornamented with cherubs' heads. On the knob there is a characteristic inscription in Slavonic : "I, Stephen Voevod, by the grace of God Hospodar of Moldavia, son of Bogdan Voevod, made this liturgical fan of mine at the Zographou Monastery of Mount Athos, 30th July 1488."

III. ICONS AND PORTRAITS.

Frontispiece. *Saint Athanasius' icon,* on which Voevod Vladislav, the donor, and his wife, Princess Anna, are shown in mediæval costumes. Second half of the XIVth century.

7 *Saint Mary* with crown of gold and precious stones. Under the nimbus, rows of pearls. The gift of Princess Helen Bassarab. First half of the XVIIth century.

8 *Fresco portraits* of Neagoe Bassarab Voevod and his son Dionysius, represented in rather curious attires. First quarter of the XVIth century.

9 *Portrait of Constantine Brancovanu,* bearing upon the right the emblem of Wallachia and on the left the inscription :

Constantinus Brankovan Supremus Valachiae Transalpinae Princeps
Aetis 42 Ao Dni 1696.

---

[1] VOEVOD the official Roumanian title given to the reigning princes of Moldavia and Wallachia.

10 *Votive icon of Joseph the Moldavian* ; thus it is mentioned by an English traveller.[1] Indeed, one finds the name in a Greek inscription between the two figures. As for the quality of Moldavian, one can deduce it from the costumes as well as from the local tradition.

11 *Mural painting.* The builders of Vlasiu Monastery, Mount Pindus : Constantine the son and Kir George, two Wallachia noblemen ; dated 1644.

12 *Christ enthroned.* Icon painted by Theodor of Bucharest, in 1717.

13 *Portrait of Nicolas Mavrogheni*, Voevod of Wallachia ; 1786-90.

IV. RELIQUARIES AND CASKETS.

14 *Silver reliquary* in oblong form, with five turrets, containing the arm of John Chrysostom. Embellished by Prince Constantine Brancovanu in 1691.

15 *Casket* to be carried on the priest's shoulder whilst going round with the incensor. In silver, beautifully enamelled. Its inscription bears witness to having been presented by Prince Matthew and his wife, Princess Helen Bassarab, 1644.

16 *Reliquary* in the shape of a Gospel. It accompanied a grant of money made in 1626 by Prince Lapushneanu of Wallachia, whose coat-of-arms is seen under the jewelled cross on the right-hand side.

17 *Reliquary* with the head of Saint Haralambus, which was sent by Prince Vladislav of Wallachia in 1488. The casket itself in silver filigree is of later date.

18 *Casket of the Wallachian Hospodar Matthew Bassarab* ; first half of XVIIth century. Undoubtedly one of the most interesting reliques, for its characteristic blending of both Byzantine and Gothic traits. Robert Curzon thus describes it :

"The material is silver gilt, but the admirable and singular style of the workmanship gives it a value far surpassing its intrinsic worth. The roof is covered with five domes of gold ; on each side it has sixteen recesses, in which are portraits of the saints in *niello*, and at each end there are eight others. All the windows are enriched in open-work tracery of a strange sort of Gothic pattern, unlike anything in Europe. It is altogether a wonderful and precious monument of ancient art, the production of an almost unknown country, rich, quaint, and original in its design and execution, and is indeed one of the most curious objects on Mount Athos."[2]

V. EMBROIDERIES.

They comprise various pieces for ecclesiastical use :

19 *Funeral pall or Epitaphion*, following in general lines a certain type consecrated by

[1] "A Description of the historic monuments of Cyprus, studies in the Archæology and Architecture of the island, with illustrations from measured drawings and photographs," Nicosia, 1912.
[2] *Visits to Monasteries in the Levant*, p. 395, London, 1916.

tradition : Christ lies on the bier—his head being supported by the sorrowful mother. With her are Mary of Magdala and the other Mary. At the foot there are seen John the Evangelist and Joseph of Arimathea. Two angels stand on the sides with liturgical fans in their hands. All the figures are finely worked in gold and silver threads upon a red velvet. Besides the border of Greek lettering, an inscription under the bier says that the Epitaphion had been bequeathed to the Holy Sepulchre in the year 1614 by Scarlat and his wife Balasha, whose portrait is shown in the lower corner on the right.

20 *Epitaphion*. This being of a later date—executed at Iassy, Moldavia, in 1792—introduces as ornamentation the Cross as well as the Instruments of Passion.

    Epitaphioi, concerned with the Assumption of Virgin Mary, are likewise made on a traditional pattern. The body of Mary lies on the bier. Nearby, among lamenting apostles, stands Christ holding the soul of the Holy Mother in the shape of a babe. All are in accordance with the model represented in such old pieces as the Pala of St. Mark and the Ivory of the Ravenna Museum ; save for the two figures under the dead Virgin. They illustrate a later legend to the effect that, when somebody wanted to push down the bier, an angel appeared and cut his arms.

21/22 Both exquisitely done with regard to the expression of the faces, upon green and red backgrounds. The inscribed gifts of the Mavrocordatos ; second half of the XVIIIth century.

23 *Chasuble*. White silk with the heads of the Evangelists embroidered thereon ; coloured borders. The donor is Prince Michael Sutzu ; 1795.

24 *Stole*. Encircled Evangelists with vine decoration. Greek inscription : "The Hand of Ioasaf Constantine, Bishop." End of the XVIIIth century.

25 *Inscribed stole*. Rich flowery ornamentation in gold. The offering of Sherban Cantacuzene, great Wallachian dignitary, in 1708.

26 *Icon cover*, representing Christ's descent into Hell ; XVIIth century.

27 *Stole*, representing the twelve Evangelists, with Slavonic inscription that it was given by Prince and Princess George Stephen of Moldavia ; 1652.

28 *Stole* of more primitive character, bequeathed by Peter Raresh Voevod ; 1546.

29 *Epigonation*. Upon a red stuff are embroidered in gold and silver various figures, with Christ in the centre, descending into Hell. The date is ҂зрм҃д = 7144 (that is, the Creation year, corresponding to our 1635) ; whilst a Slavonic inscription tells us of the donor, Zupan Chrysos, and his wife, Zupanitza Gherghina, Wallachian nobles.

Saint Peter says that Jesus Christ in the interval between His death and resurrection descended into Hell, awaking and lifting up Adam. This impressed the people of the Eastern Greek Church to the extent of reaching a symbolical meaning : The first man that sinned was the first to be redeemed. The scene, mentioned in connection with No. 29, is very often represented on the back covers. As for the Gospels, we have to point out that the majority of them display a high artistic quality, being the work of worthy illuminators, attracted to the Moldo-wallachian courts by most generous and appreciative patrons. The names of the latter are usually inscribed on the Gospels, in addition to explanations that they were made for their souls' sake and to imprecations such as the following : "Whoever would remove from its place the present Gospel, let him be anathematised by the Almighty and by the Holy Mother and by the Holy Fathers of Nicæa, and let him in the frightful Judgment be ranked with Juda and Satana."

Many of these Gospels are modelled upon lost Byzantine originals ; so that they maintain for us and perpetuate some aspects of a precious ecclesiastical art. And, in going along the lines of their development, one can easily notice how, after strong Persian and Syrian influences, there appears in them a freer breath, a delightfully simple impress of native elements.

30 *Gospel* of Prince Tchiobanu. Splendid covers in silver—on the front side the Crucifix ; on the other, the Birth of Saint John the Baptist. And under this a dedicatory Slavonic inscription of the Prince, his wife, his son and his daughters, whose figures are clearly distinguished from amongst saints and flowers. First half of the XVIth century.

31 *Manuscript* of Greek Gospel, presented to the Vatopedi Monastery, Mount Athos, in 1598, by the Moldavian boyar Cratchiun, as pointed out in its Slavonic preface.

32 *Gospel in Slavonic characters*, written by a certain Priest Nicolas, "at the command of the Voevod", as the inscription adds, without giving his name.

33 *Beaten bronze cover*, showing on one side the Resurrection, on the other Saint Nicolas, masterfully carved ; and round the border a Slavonic inscription, dated 1551 : "This Gospel was made and bound by Helen, Wife and Princess of the late Peter Voevod . . ."

34 *Beaten bronze cover*. Much like the above. On one side, instead of Saint Nicolas, one meets with the Mother of God amongst angels and saints. It belonged to the son of Princess Helen, Stephen Raresh.

35 *Gospel cover in archaic style*. It shows under the scene of the Transfiguration the figures of Prince Alexander, of his wife Catherine, and his son, about whom speaks the inscription. Second half of the XVIth century.

7

36 *Gospel with heavy beaten bronze cover*, showing ornamented medallions of saints. On the back side, the Moldavian emblem and the dedicatory inscription on the part of Prince Jeremia Movila, 1598. There are inside illuminated head-pages and borders as well as a beautiful image of St. John.

37 *Another Gospel.* The piety of Princess Catherine, wife of Jeremia Movila, is responsible for the sending of another illuminated Gospel to the East.

38 *Gospel* written by the Calligrapher Matthew in 1599, whilst abbot of a monastery in Moldavia.

39 *Second Gospel* by the Calligrapher Matthew, eleven years later, in 1610, when he became Bishop of Buzau, as the inscription says, "by the desire and the expenses of the highest and most honourable Doamna[1] Catalina of Craiova".

40 *A third Gospel* by the same I found at Ianina, Epirus. It exhibits an obvious Renaissance influence.

41 *Gospel by Metropolite Luke.* One of the most beautiful. The whole work in the minutest detail testifies to a very skilful and experienced illuminator. The cover of beaten bronze, finely carved, displays a church on the back half. At the end a Greek inscription : "This Godly and Holy Gospel was written by my hand the humble metropolite of Ungro-wallachia Luke in the days of our most honourable and blessed Prince Radul Voevod, in the year 7124" (that is, 1616 A.D.).

42 *Gospel* written by the Monk Porfirie, in 1633, with intricate, carpet-like ornamentation which indicates Eastern influences.

43 *Beaten bronze covered Gospel* of Prince Matthew Bassarab ; dated 1642. It contains a full-size portrait of the donor and of his wife, Princess Helen.

44 The same Prince Matthew Bassarab bequeathed to the Holy Sepulchre another Gospel, which is very interesting for its primitive simplicity of the coloured scenes. The illuminator seems to be inspired now and again by the peasant life around him.

45 *Wood-covered Slavonic Gospel.* Only three pages at the beginning are in parchment. At the fifth page there is a curiously ornamented border, comprising within an inscription to the effect that the Gospel was made at the command of Dabija Voevod in 1665.

46 *Beaten bronze cover* of a Gospel bequeathed by Prince Brancovanu to the Patmos Monastery. End of the XVIIth century.

47 This is also a wood-covered Slavonic Gospel, with only six pages in parchment. An inscription at the end gives the name of Monk Michael as the writer of it in 1655.

[1] *Doamna*—the title given to the wife of the reigning Prince of Moldavia and Wallachia, who besides being called Voevod, was usually himself addressed as *Domn*.

1

ALTAR CROSSES AND HOLY-WATER VESSELS

1. *Gilt Bronze Cross of Istrati Dabija Voevod, XVIIth Century.*

Holy Sepulchre's Treasury, Jerusalem.

2. *Wooden Cross, dated 1776.*

Lower Part of the Wooden Cross.

Zitza Monastery, Epirus.

II

3. *Altar Cross.*

Zitza Monastery, Epirus.

12

4. *Holy-Water Vessel of George Stephen Voevod, 1656.*

Holy Sepulchre's Treasury, Jerusalem.

13

2

LITURGICAL FANS. PIΠÌΔIA

5. *Liturgical Fan of Peter Voevod and his son Radul.*

Lower Part of the Liturgical Fan with the Portraits of the Donors.

Holy Sepulchre's Treasury, Jerusalem.

6. *Liturgical Fan, 1488.*

Patmos Monastery.

16

3

ICONS AND PORTRAITS

7. *Icon of Saint Mary, XVIIth Century.*

Chiliandari Monastery, Mount Athos.

18

8. *Fresco Portraits of Neagoe Bassarab Voevod and his son Dionysius, XVIth Century.*

Dionisiu Monastery, Mount Athos.

19

9. *Portrait of Constantine Brancovanu, 1696.*

Mount Sinai Monastery.
(Now in the possession of Princess Bibescu.)

10. *Votive Icon of Joseph the Moldavian.*

Church of Faneromeny, Cyprus.

11. *Mural Painting, dated* 1644.

Vlasiu Monastery, Mount Pindus.

12. *Christ Enthroned,* 1717.

Spilià Monastery, Mount Pindus.

13. *Portrait of Nicolas Mavrogheni, 1786–90.*

Ethnographic Museum, Athens.

4

RELIQUARIES AND CASKETS

14. *Silver Reliquary*, 1691.

Lavra Monastery, Mount Athos.

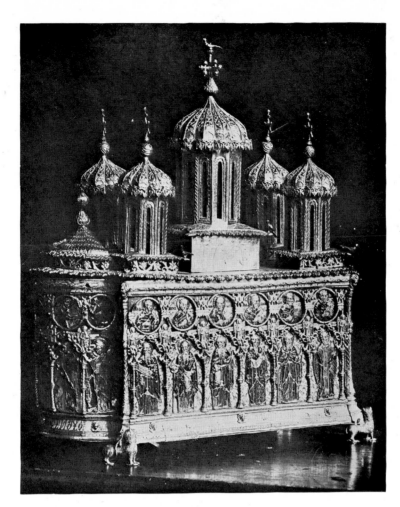

15. *Enamelled Silver Casket, 1644.*

Lavra Monastery, Mount Athos.

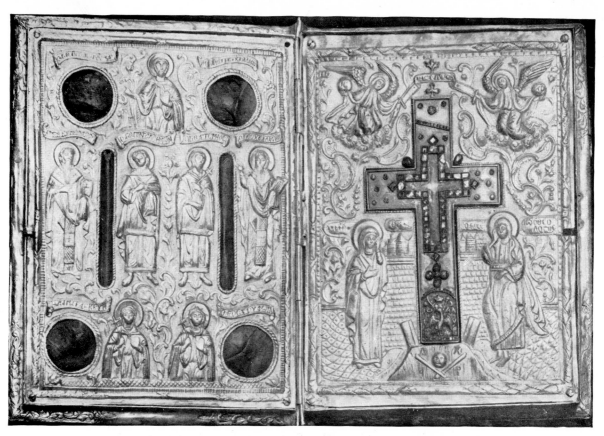

16. *Gospel-shaped Reliquary, 1626.*

Dokiariou Monastery, Mount Athos.

Head of Saint Haralambus in the same Reliquary when Opened.

Saint Stephen's Monastery, Meteores.

17. Silver Reliquary.

35

18. *Casket of Mixed Byzantine and Gothic Styles, XVIIth Century.*

Dionisiu Monastery, Mount Athos.

5

EMBROIDERIES

19. *Epitaphion, dated* 1614.

Holy Sepulchre's Treasury, Jerusalem.

20. *Epitaphion*, 1792.

Makhaera's Monastery, Cyprus.

21. *Death of Virgin Mary, XVIIIth Century.*

Church of the Virgin's Tomb, Jerusalem.

22. *The Mavrocordatos' Epitaphion, XVIIIth Century.*

Tomb of the Holy Virgin.

41

23. *Chasuble of Prince Michael Sutzu, 1795.*

Church of the Greek Patriarchate, Istambul.

42

24. *Prince Mavrogheni's Stole, XVIIIth Century.*

Church of Ekatontapoliani, Paros.

25. *Inscribed Stole of Sherban Cantacuzene, 1708.*

Church of Greek Patriarchate, Istambul.

44

26. *Icon Cover.*

Holy Sepulchre's Treasury, Jerusalem.

27. *Stole of Prince George Stephen, 1652.*

Holy Sepulchre's Treasury, Jerusalem.

47

27. *Stole of Prince George Stephen, 1652.*

Holy Sepulchre's Treasury, Jerusalem.

49

28. *Stole of Peter Raresh Voevod,* 1546.

Esphigmenou Monastery, Mount Athos.

29. *Epigonation.*

National Museum of Sofia.

50

6

GOSPELS AND GOSPEL-COVERS

30. *Gospel of Prince Tchiobanu, XVIth Century.*
Monastery of Dionisiu, Mount Athos.

Miniature from the same Gospel.

Monastery of Dionisiu, Mount Athos.

30. *Illuminated Page from Prince Tchiobani's Gospel.*

31. *Greek Gospel of the boyar Cratchiun, 1598.*

It belonged to the Monastery of Vatopedi, Mount Athos. Now at the National Library, Athens.

Initial Letter of the Cratchiun Gospel, 1598.

32. *Page from the Gospel of Priest Nicolas.*

Saint Sepulchre's Library.

Back Cover.

Front Cover.

33. *Beaten Bronze Cover of Princess Helen's Gospel,* 1551.

Holy Sepulchre's Treasury, Jerusalem.

56

34. *Illuminated Page from the Gospel of Prince Stephen Raresh, XVIth Century.*

Holy Sepulchre's Treasury, Jerusalem.

34. *Illuminated Page from the Gospel of Prince Stephen Raresh, XVIth Century.*

Holy Sepulchre's Treasury, Jerusalem.

Back Cover.

Front Cover.

35. *Cover of Prince Alexander's Gospel, XVIth Century.*

Sinai Monastery.

35. *Page from Prince Alexander's Gospel, XVIth Century.*

Sinai Monastery.

62

36. *Illuminated Page from Prince Jeremia Movila's Gospel*, 1598.

Sinai Monastery.

Front Cover. 36. *Bronze Covers of Prince Jeremia Movila's Gospel,* 1598. *Back Cover.*

Sinai Monastery.

65

36. *Illuminated Page from Prince Jeremia Movila's Gospel, 1598.*

Sinai Monastery.

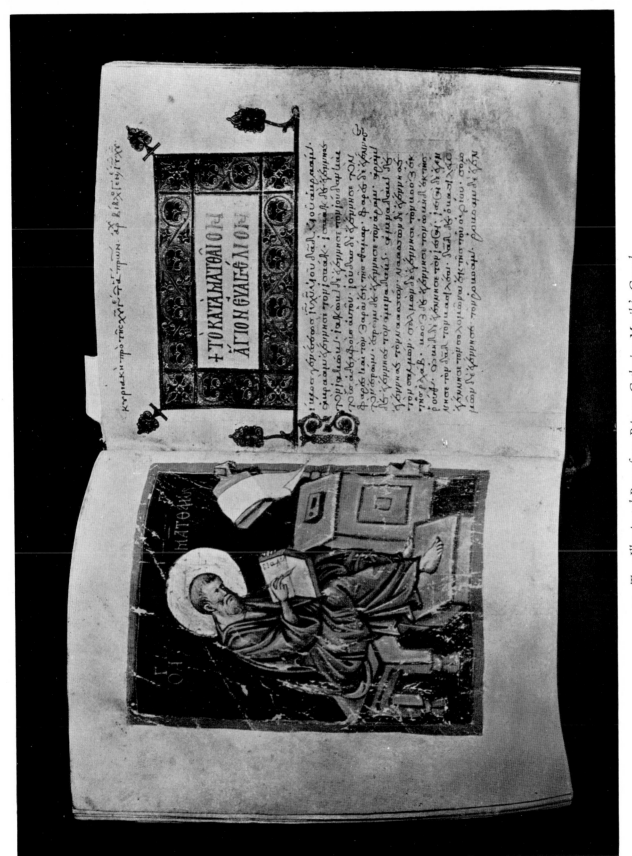

37. *Two Illuminated Pages from Princess Catherine Movila's Gospel.*

Koutloumoush Monastery, Mount Athos.

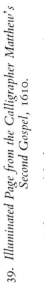

39. *Illuminated Page from the Calligrapher Matthew's Second Gospel,* 1610.

Holy Sepulchre's Treasury, Jerusalem.

38. *Illuminated Page from the Calligrapher Matthew's Gospel,* 1599.

Mar-Sabba Monastery.

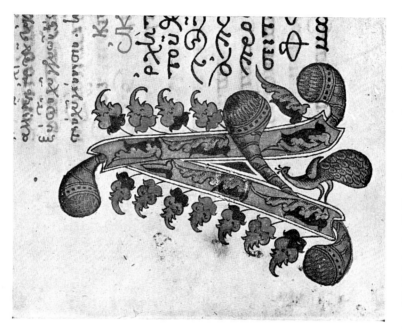

39. *Illuminated Initials in the Calligrapher Matthew's Second Gospel, 1610. Holy Sepulchre's Treasury, Jerusalem.*

70

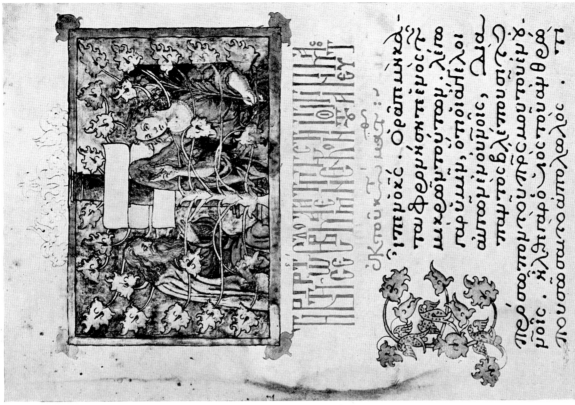

40. *Two Illuminated Pages from Bishop Matthew's Gospel.*
Iaṅina, Epirus.

71

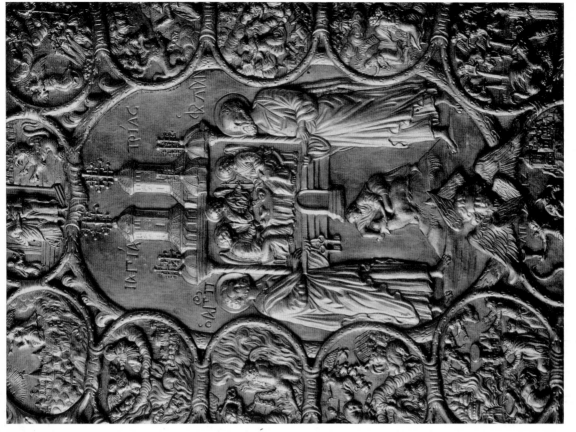

Back Cover.

Front Cover.

41. *Covers of Metropolite Luke's Gospel, 1616.*
Holy Sepulchre's Treasury, Jerusalem.

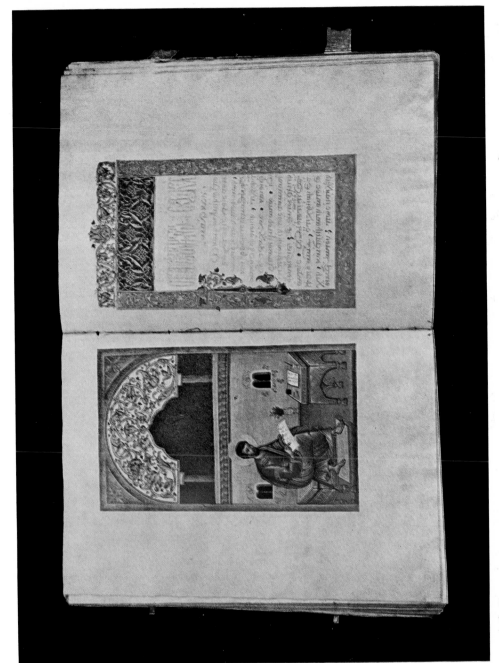

41. *Illuminated Page from Metropolite Luke's Gospel.*

Holy Sepulchre's Treasury, Jerusalem.

73

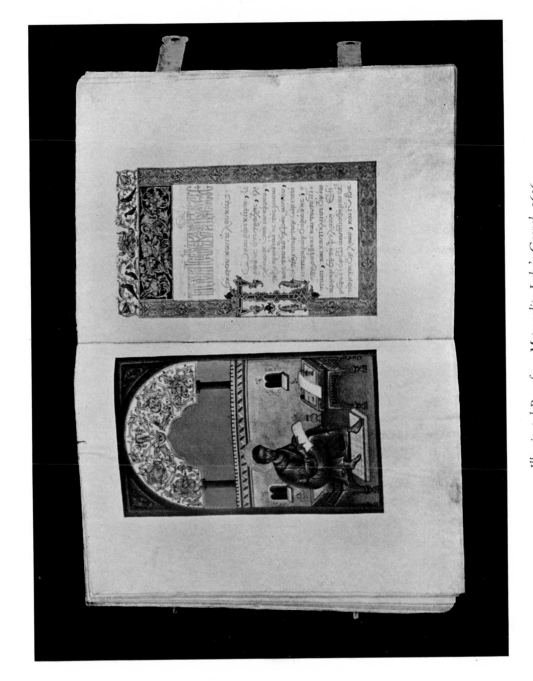

41. *Illuminated Page from Metropolite Luke's Gospel, 1616.*

Holy Sepulchre's Treasury, Jerusalem.

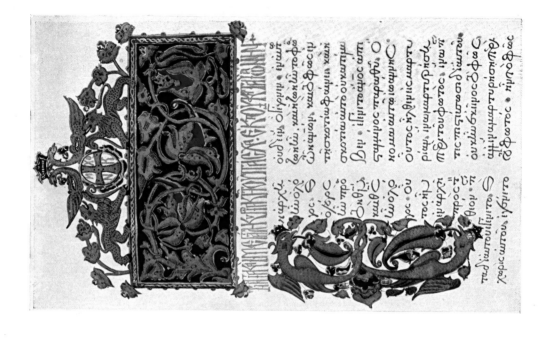

42. Illuminated Pages from Monk Porfirie's Gospel, 1633.

Holy Sepulchre's Treasury, Jerusalem.

78

42. Miniatures from Monk Porfirie's Gospel, 1633.

Holy Sepulchre's Treasury, Jerusalem.

80

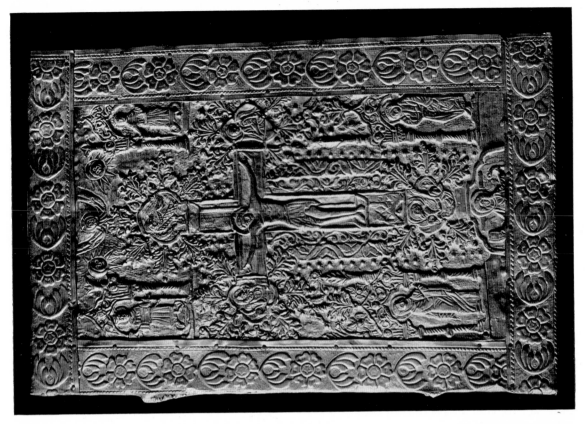

Back Cover.

43. *Covers of Prince Matthew Bassarab's Gospel, 1642.*
Holy Sepulchre's Treasury, Jerusalem.

Front Cover.

81

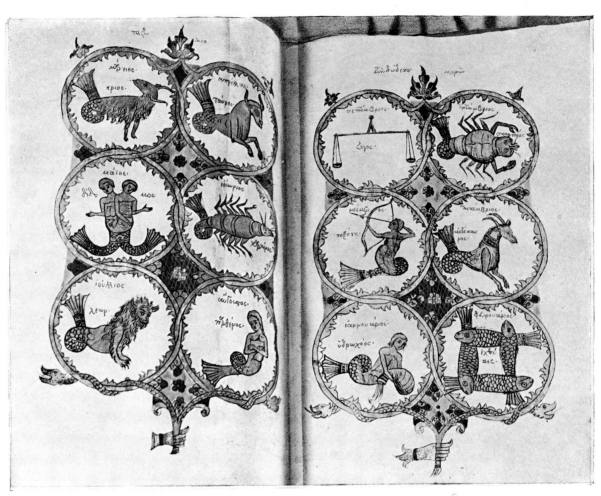

43. *The Zodiac in Prince Matthew Bassarab's Gospel,* 1642.
Holy Sepulchre's Treasury, Jerusalem.

43. *Miniature from Prince Matthew Bassarab's Gospel, 1642.*

Holy Sepulchre's Treasury, Jerusalem.

43. *Illuminated Page and Miniature from Prince Matthew Bassarab's Gospel, 1642.*

Holy Sepulchre's Treasury, Jerusalem.

44. *Illuminated Page from Prince Matthew Bassarab's Second Gospel,* 1643.

Holy Sepulchre's Treasury, Jerusalem.

44. *Headpieces from Prince Matthew Bassarab's Second Gospel*, 1643.

Holy Sepulchre's Treasury, Jerusalem.

44. *Illuminated Pages from Prince Matthew Bassarab's Second Gospel*, 1643.

Holy Sepulchre's Treasury, Jerusalem.

44. *Miniatures from Prince Matthew Bassarab's Second Gospel,* 1643.

Holy Sepulchre's Treasury, Jerusalem.

93

44. Illuminated Pages from Prince Matthew Bassarh's Second Gospel, 1643.

Holy Sepulchre's Treasury, Jerusalem.

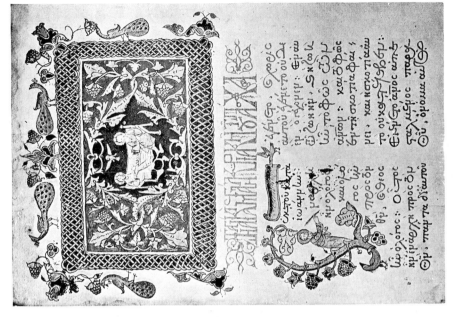

44. Illuminated Page from Prince Matthew Bassarab's
Second Gospel, 1643.

44. The Zodiac from Prince Matthew Bassarab's
Second Gospel, 1643.

Holy Sepulchre's Treasury, Jerusalem.

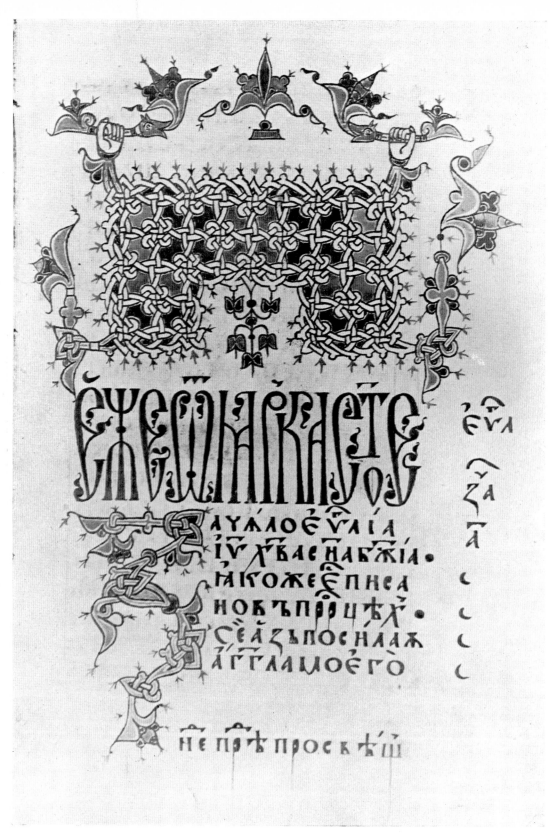

45. Illuminated Page from Dabija Voevod's Gospel in Slavonic, 1665.

45. *Illuminated Pages from Dabija Voevod's Gospel in Slavonic*, 1665.

Holy Sepulchre's Treasury, Jerusalem.

97

46. *Beaten Bronze Cover of Prince Brancovanu's Gospel, XVIIth Century.*

Patmos Monastery.

98

47. Miniatures from Monk Michael's Gospel, 1655.

99

INDEX

The Vlasiu Monastery, Mount Pindus.